C000121514

IMAGES OF ENGLAND

Frodsham and Helsby

IMAGES OF ENGLAND

Frodsham and Helsby

Frodsham and District Local History Group

NONSUCH

First published 1995
This new pocket edition 2005
Images unchanged from first edition

Nonsuch Publishing Limited
The Mill, Brimscombe Port,
Stroud, Gloucestershire, GL5 2QG
www.nonsuch-publishing.com

British Library Cataloguing in Publication Data.
A catalogue record for this book is available from the British Library.

ISBN 1-84588-147-8

Typesetting and origination by Nonsuch Publishing Limited
Printed in Great Britain by Oaklands Book Services Limited

Contents

Acknowledgements

Frodsham & District Local History Group wish to acknowledge the contribution made by the photographic collections of the late Mr Joe Barker and the descendants of the Wright Family, represented by Mrs Christine Hewlett.

We are also indebted to many people who, over a considerable number of years, have donated photographs to the Local History Group. Without their help, this book could not have been produced.

Editorial Committee

Norma Duncan, Jean Forster, Jim Harvey,
Bill Hawkin, Dorothy Smith, Beryl Wainwright

The Cholmondeley Arms, Church Street, *c.* 1900. Previously, this had been a beer house known as the Albert Inn, owned by the Atlas Brewery, as the advertisement on the gable of the adjoining building testifies. In 1900 the licensee was Mr. F.M. Payne, who only stayed two years, but his successors, Mr and Mrs Howard Baker remained in charge until 1921.

Introduction

The twin villages of Frodsham and Helsby have a history which extends back more than two thousand years, when late Stone Age man established a flint-knapping factory, making flint-tipped implements and weapons, on what is now a field near Harrol Edge Reservoir. Iron Age people followed and established hill forts on Helsby Hill, Woodhouses Hill and at Bradley.

The Romans came and left 400 years later followed by the first people to settle on the site. These were Saxons whose leader (named either Frod or Froda) established a Ham at the foot of the hill which became part of the Anglo-Saxon Kingdom of Mercia.

About the year 900 AD a band of Vikings from Ireland, led by a Norseman by the name of Ingemund, crossed the Irish Sea and settled in the Wirral Peninsula. Helsby seems to have been the eastern outpost of this wave of settlement, where the Norsemen built their village on a narrow shelf of land between the hill and the undrained marshes. They called it Hjallr-by-the village on the ledge. Perhaps the old fort on the hilltop was an added advantage for this outpost of the Norse community. The area was wasted by William's Normans in 1070, yet two centuries later Ranulf III, the Norman Earl of Chester granted Frodsham a Charter which made it a Borough.

At the beginning of the seventeenth century, the powerful Savage family became, by purchase, Lords of the Manor of Frodsham, whereupon existing leases were declared void and a process of rack renting was begun, with rents being increased year by year. This resulted in many violent confrontations between the inhabitants and the Savage family's strong-arm men from the Castle. The Castle was destroyed by fire in 1654 and it remained a ruin until it was sold to Daniel Ashley in 1750.

The Ashley's demolished the castle ruins and erected upon the site a house called Park Place which they occupied until 1841 when it became the home of Capt. Harry Heron. Then, in 1851, it was purchased by Joseph Stubs, a wealthy Warrington manufacturer who immediately set about reconstructing and extending the house to approximately its present size. He engaged Edward Kemp, who had created this country's first municipal park in Birkenhead, to lay out the grounds and gardens. In 1861 the estate was purchased by Edward Abbott Wright, an Oldham mill-owner, whose family remained in residence for many years.

The railway came to Frodsham in 1850 and the area's agricultural products – vegetable and animal – began to be exported through Frodsham station. Potato baskets were made by the thousand by a local firm. Fruit from the area was made into jams and a creamery was established near Frodsham Station. Bone meal and similar fertilisers were manufactured down by the River Weaver at Frodsham Bridge, where a port and flour mills had also been established. The railway also attracted the town's first commuters – factory owners and managers from the surrounding towns.

The old Turnpikes became quite unable to cope with the vastly increased number of motor vehicles which began making their way on to the roads after the First World War. This was particularly noticeable during the summer months when holiday traffic from South Lancashire made its way to Chester and North Wales by way of the A56 and traffic jams in both Frodsham and Helsby were a common occurrence.

The situation became even worse in the post-Second World War period when the traffic load rose to over 21,000 vehicles in a 16-hour day. A campaign for a by-pass was launched and a demonstration in 1964 managed to involve the then Prime Minister, Sir Alec Douglas-Home as he passed through Helsby. Eventually, in 1971, the M56 opened and the flood of vehicles diminished to a more reasonable level.

The villages in our area, once part of the Runcorn Union, divided from the urban part of the area to form part of the Runcorn Rural District from 1894 to 1974. Frodsham at first had two Parish Councils – the Township and the Lordship Councils – but these were combined in 1936 into a single Civil Parish. 1 April 1974 saw the demise of the Rural District Council and the emergence of Vale Royal Council, covering the whole of central Cheshire. Frodsham's Parish Council has now become a Town Council with a mayor instead of a chairman.

Although change has been taking place in our villages during the whole of their history, the greatest has occurred during the last hundred years when the area has been transformed from a mostly agricultural community, where everything moved at the pace of the horse, to today's commuter township. Such industry as Frodsham possessed has all but disappeared. Even the great BICC factory in Helsby no longer exists, a new Tesco store, low-cost housing and offices being proposed for the site.

It is fortunate that, since the middle of the nineteenth century, photographs have been taken and many of these now form the Frodsham and District Local History Group's photographic archive. A selection of these has been made to illustrate the villages in former times. It is hoped these images will interest our younger readers and remind their elders of their past.

One

Streets and Buildings

Church Street, c. 1910. On the left is Lloyd's butcher's shop. A chauffeur-driven limousine waits outside J.G. Kydd's grocers shop while madame orders her week's supplies inside. On the right is Collinson's grocers. Mr Collinson was once an employee of Joseph Kydd, but set up in opposition almost opposite!

View from the Church Tower, 1900. The buildings on the right were once the Roebuck Inn, built in 1669. Later it became a farm and today it is a private residence. The large house in the centre is Hillsboro, which was once Carpenter's School for Gentlemen's Sons. During the Second World War it was Frodsham's Food Office, but has now been demolished and the site used for residential development.

Church Cottages, Overton, c. 1900. These cottages were situated in what is now the church car park and were demolished in 1927. Betty Mercer had a sweet shop and became famous for her humbugs. Mrs Knight followed in her footsteps and can be seen here, standing in the shop doorway. Next door was Mrs Martha Hoose, who was a midwife. The Ring o' Bells Inn opposite, was a yeoman's cottage before the Civil War when it was known as Hough's Cottage after its owner, Joseph Hough. He sold the property for £22 in 1692. It is now owned by a well-known brewery.

School Lane, Overton, c. 1900. On the left, is the now-vanished Pump Cottage. To the right, Overton Cottage which was probably Miss Singleton's Boarding School for Young Ladies at that time. On the opposite side of Hillside Road is Hawthorn Cottage which was burnt down, whilst on the hilltop can be seen the buildings of the skating rink, which were used as an Auxiliary Hospital during the First World War.

Flower and Pump Cottages, c. 1900. Situated at the junction of School Lane and Hillside Road – then known as Back Lane – are these two cottages. Flower Cottage still remains today, but Pump Cottage and its pump have long since gone. The cupola of Frodsham Endowed Boys' School and Overton School House can just be seen in the background.

Overton in 1900. Overton Cottage on the right. Is that Miss Singleton standing at the door? The sandstone building between the Bull's Head and the Ring o' Bells has gone now to provide car parking. At that time it offered storage for bicycles.

Thatched Cottages, Howey Lane, in the early 1930s. These once stood at the top of Pinmill Brow, just where the present street nameplate for Pinmill Close is now situated.

Overton Hill in the 1930s. A walker perches perilously on a rocky outcrop. In the distance the War Memorial, Mersey View and the long-lost helter-skelter are just visible. Notice the lack of trees on the hill, even at this date. The hill is now, however, covered with trees.

DANCING ON THE GREEN – MERSEY VIEW.

Mersey View Pleasure Grounds in the early years of the twentieth century. Dancing on the green, rides on donkeys, swing boats, slides on the helter-skelter, to say nothing of fresh air. All manner of refreshments were available at that time.

Left: Erection of Helter Skelter, 1908. Built for Mrs Parker-Hoose by the local builders, JG Davies & Co. The men in the photograph, from top to bottom are: Messrs H Ormsby, S Burkhill, T Corker, E Corker, J Garner, S Gilgrist, W Walker and the man at the bottom is T Youd.

Below: Caves, Manley Road, *c.* 1900. The caves were a popular destination for an afternoon walk in Edwardian times. A small natural cave had been enlarged to obtain sand for spreading on cottage floors. The last person to sell sand from the caves was Billy Tweedle about 1895.

Caves near Overton Hills, Frodsham.

14

Five Crosses Smithy, c. 1900. The smithy stood in what would now be the middle of the road at the Kingsley Road/Manley Road junction. It was owned by Frederick Houghton, who lived in Townfield Lane. The large wooden building in the background was Joseph Berrington's wheelwright's workshop. Joseph described himself as a Wheelwright, Coach Builder and Blacksmith.

Davies's Baker's Shop & Virginia Cottage, Five Crosses, c. 1900. John Henry Davies was a grocer and baker and lived with his family of five daughters and two sons in Virginia Cottage, next door to the shop. Here we see them on a sunny afternoon, dressed in their Sunday best with the ladies carrying parasols.

Aubrey House, Bellemonte Road, c. 1860. Samson Harvey was Frodsham's local chemist with a shop in Church Street. He was an early photographer and many of our earliest photographs of Frodsham were taken by him. This is almost certainly one of them. The dress of the ladies and the tall hat of the gentleman are typical of the period.

Churchfield House, Church Street, 1937. Churchfield House was the residence of the Cotgreave family, who were butchers with a shop in Church Street. The flag is probably flying in commemoration of the coronation of King George VI and Queen Elizabeth. The surrounding land has now been developed for housing purposes and the drive with the gate is now Churchfield Road.

Above: Upper Church Street, *c.* 1900. We are looking up Church Street with what is now the Model Shop on our right. Higher up is the turning into Kingsway. Just out of picture on our left are Whitehall Cottages. The view has hardly changed at all. Are those boys holding snowballs?

Right: Terraced Houses, Church Street, *c.* 1900. The cyclist carefully negotiates the treacherous road surface, passing Oliphant's general shop. Further up, past the two white cottages, is Lockett's greengrocer's shop which Edgar Brereton was later to occupy. All this property was demolished to make way for the Eddisbury Square shopping development.

Church Street, *c.* 1900. The projecting gas lamp and the "Perth Dye Works" advertisement are at the point where Garner's Lane joins Church Street. The glass fronted wooden building, which houses the cobbler's workshop obscures the white cottages occupied by the Bibby (basket-making) family. Then we have the new block of shops which extends to Kydd's Wynt and the Girls' School. A horseman rides uphill past the entrance to the railway goods yard towards Sandfields.

Opposite above: Williams's Sweet Shop. This building can be seen in very early photographs of Frodsham when it formed part of Nield's smithy. The shop door was once a stable-type door.

Opposite below: The Grand Cinema, Church Street, *c.* 1930. The Grand was opened in November 1923, under the management of Mr Tom Fylde, when silent films were shown. The first Talkie was *Under the Greenwood Tree*, shown in 1928. The site is now Premier Bridge convenience store. The two little shops beyond were converted from a disused cricket pavilion. The nearer was a sweet shop known as "Toffee Roberts" and the other was Jimmy Clarke's saddlery.

Church Street from Main Street junction, *c.* 1900. From 1822 until 1845, the Golden Lion was known as the White Hart. It then belonged to Mather's Brewery, Penketh. It passed to Gaskarth's of Altrincham in 1879 and to Samuel Smith in 1967. In mediaeval times the site was a Burgage Plot and there is a deed dated 1361 in existence whereby it was granted to Henry Torfote, one of Frodsham's up-and-coming men at that time.

Opposite above: Lower Church Street, *c.* 1910. The Bear's Paw Hotel, on the far side of Main Street, looks up towards the railway bridge. On our left is Rothwell's Ironmongers (later Tom Pollard's and now the Betting Shop) and the Golden Lion is on the Main Street corner. Pollard Bros. drapers shop is on the right, then Hancock's butchers, Clarke's grocery store, and Earlam's chemists shop. These have now been replaced by a travel agency, a bridal shop, Haifax and Cheshire Building Societies and Moss parmacy. The beautiful chestnut tree at the end of Station Lane was removed when the A&N Rubber Company built their factory on the site. It is now the Wellspring Centre.

Opposite below: Conversion of Crosbie House to Draper's Shop, *c.* 1900. Crosbie House, was once the residence of William Crosbie, a Liverpool businessman, who was a partner in the Salt Works at Frodsham Bridge. Later, part of the building was used as a boys' school – "Mr. Church's Academy" – and part as a draper's shop by John Guest Williams. The shop thrived and was later inherited by his two apprentices, James Proud and Edwin Pollard. It was then extended into the rest of Crosbie House and became Pollard Bros.

The Whalebone Inn, Netherton, c. 1860. This old hostelry has long-since vanished, as has its 1895 successor. At this time the licensee was Thomas Bate, whose sons John and William succeeded him. It was once known as the Fishbone. The bone on the front of the inn is said to have come from a whale, washed up on to Frodsham Marsh at high tide. The licence has now been transferred to nearby Netherton Hall.

Opposite above: Millbank Cottages, Main Street, c. 1900. These seventeenth-century cottages adjoined the brick-built Volunteer Inn public house. Although in recent years they lay empty, became semi-derelict and had to be demolished, the planning permission for the adjoining land required them to be rebuilt in exactly the same form. This has been done with some success. Among the people standing in their front gardens are Messrs Ellison, Corker, Calveley and Jack Edge, who was then licensee of the Volunteer Inn.

Opposite below: The Fold, Marsh Green, c. 1900. Here are some more of Frodsham's long-lost thatched cottages, and three of their inhabitants. These were situated near the point where Marsh Lane joins Hare Lane.

Pair of Cottages, West end of Main Street, c. 1860. We know this is one of Samson Harvey's photographs, because the original has his name embossed on the back. The cottages were replaced with a row of terraced houses later in the century.

West end of Main Street, c. 1900. The terrace houses which replaced the cottages in the previous photograph are on the left and beyond, we can see the bulk of the Bourne Methodist Chapel. The white cottages on the right were burned down in 1902. Beyond them is a pair of three-storey houses, where Mrs Yard had her boarding house, which in the 1850's accommodated Sarah Bristow and her sister Eleanor, who taught at the new National School in Church Street. The Cheshire Cheese pub comes next, then the shop and beyond two more white cottages, where Frodsham's original telephone exchange was situated.

West Bank Cottages, Main Street, 1902. We see them the morning after the fire which marked their demise. The site is now occupied by a modern detached house.

Brookstone Cottages, Main Street, c. 1900. Externally, Brookstone Cottages have hardly changed at all during the twentieth century. It is interesting to note the manhole in the roadway, which indicates that not only sewers, but a piped water supply was now available.

Cattle in Main Street, 1946. It seems remarkable that as late as 1946 cattle could still be seen making their way along Main Street. It would be a risky procedure in 2005!

Cruck building, Main Street, 1900. This was one of the last cruck buildings still remaining in Frodsham. The site is now occupied by Coward's butcher's shop. The building to the right is now a computer shop.

The Old Hall and Thatched Cottages, Main Street, 1951. We are indebted to Mr RA Collinge for a delightful sketch of this part of Main Street, which thankfully remains very much the same today.

Main Street in the 1920s. This picture is of particular interest because it shows the extent to which Frodsham's market had shrunk at that time. To-day it has grown to almost alarming proportions. Road traffic includes cars, a bus, a van and a motor-cycle and sidecar. Note also, the huge telegraph poles dominating the trees on the south side of the street.

Frodsham Post Office, Main Street, c. 1900. Frodsham's Post Office was once in the end cottage to the west of the Old Hall, but then moved across the road to what later became Lawless's Grocer's Shop next door in fact, to the present Post Office. Here we see Miss Ormerod, the Post Mistress with her assistants and two telegraph boys. The advertisements are for Stephen's Ink and picture postcards.

The Bear's Paw Hotel, Coronation Day, 1911. This old coaching-inn built in 1632, was where mail was collected and despatched before the Post Office came into being. Its name derives from the bear's paw in the coat of arms of the Savage family, Lords of the Manor of Frodsham from the early seventeenth century. With the arrival of the railway, it became The Bear's Paw & Railway Hotel until about 1905. The Youd family had it for many years and a cattle market was held on Wednesdays in the yard at the rear.

Above: The Butter Market, Main Street, *c.*1860. This is probably another Samson Harvey photograph. The stalls seem to be erected just about where the traffic lights in the centre of the town are now situated.

Left: Jacob's Ladder, Dunsdale, *c.* 1925. Jacob's Ladder was a rough flight of steps cut into the soft sandstone of Frodsham Hill. Wear and tear gradually wore them away and although this is now part of the Sandstone Trail, they have been replaced by wooden steps in a slightly different position.

Bank Top Farm, Netherton, c. 1900. A typical half-timbered Cheshire farmhouse, probably dating from the seventeenth century.

Carriage Drive, Netherton, c. 1900. In this turn of the century photograph, Hempgill stands in splendid isolation. The drive is now completely built up to the point from which this view was taken.

Rock Cottage, Chester Road, Netherton, 1952. A view of Rock Cottage from the forecourt of the Whalebone Inn. Rock Cottage remains, but the Whalebone has gone.

Black and white Cottage, Tarvin Road, c. 1900. Another old farmhouse, similar to Bank Top Farm, which still retained its thatched roof in 1900.

Iron Dish Cottage, Woodhouses, *c.* 1900. One of several tiny cottages in Godscroft Lane. It has already lost its thatched roof, although the outbuilding still has one. Note the water butt to receive water from the roof, although there was a well in the back garden.

High Street in the Snow, *c.* 1898. The Diamond Jubilee tree has not grown much since it was planted. The new Police Station is in operation, judging by the notice headed "Movement of Swine". Perhaps there had been an outbreak of swine fever in the area. Meanwhile a horse and carts plods up the Rock in the snow, and we can see another bracketed gas-lamp at the corner of Ship Street.

Rock Cottage & adjoining Cottages, High Street, *c.* 1900. The tiny cottage with a corrugated-iron roof housed Fireman (and local chimney sweep) John Willie Percival and his family of seven. There was a room in the roof reached by a ladder. The larger cottage has managed to retain its thatched roof.

Stockton House, High Street, *c.* 1900. In 1851, this was the residence of James Upton (Draper & Farmer of 50 acres) who achieved fame in the mid-nineteenth century by growing a pear weighing 15 oz. of a variety called "Sutton King". Almost certainly it was from the orchard at the rear of the property.

Half-timbered cottages, High Street, c. 1900. These sevententh-century cottages on the opposite side of the road were the subject of a Council demolition order in the 1950s. If they had managed to survive another few years, they would probably have been listed and restored with the help of government grants.

Goose Cottage, High Street, c. 1900. These two Victorian gentlemen stand outside another of Frodsham's long-lost thatched cottages. It was said to be called Goose Cottage, because geese being driven to market in Chester used the premises as an overnight stopping place. "Bed & Breakfast for Geese"?

Hutchinson's Garage, High Street, c. 1950. Arthur Hutchinson was a member of Frodsham's Fire Service and during the Second World War his taxi was used to tow a trailer pump. At this time women served in the National Fire Service and the Frodsham Women's team won a national championship using "Hutch's" taxi to tow their pump.

The British Legion Hut, High Street, 1953. Here the hut is dressed overall for the coronation celebrations in June with Mr J. Barker sen. and his two sons. Joe Barker, who collected old photographs of Frodsham is on the right. The Hut has now been demolished and replaced by a house.

Hattie Littler's Shop, Bridge Lane in the 1930's. It was well-known to the cycling fraternity in the inter-War years, as many cycling clubs would pass through Frodsham on their way to and from Chester and North Wales. She provided teas, minerals (particularly "Tizer the Appetizer!") and cigarettes. One of Frodsham's medieval cruck buildings stood on this site until the early years of the century.

Frodsham Motors, now Gates of Frodsham, in Bridge Lane in the 1950s. Frodsham Motors occupied the building fronting Bridge Lane, whilst the large buildings at the rear were the premises of Helsby & Longden's haulage firm – two Frodsham men who made good. The brick building at an angle to the road is the old Mounfield Farmhouse, isolated among all the new development. It was demolished shortly afterwards.

The stone bridge at Frodsham Bridge, *c.* 1900. The bridge was just 50 years old when this photograph was taken; it replaced the old brick bridge a few yards further down which suffered damage during the Civil War. The steam engine at Rigby's Flour Mills is in operation to judge by the plume of smoke issuing from the chimney. Joseph Ashworth's factory on the opposite bank can just be glimpsed below the bridge.

The Quay, Frodsham Bridge, c. 1900. The railway viaduct towers over the houses on the Quay and the buildings of Joseph Ashworth & Son's Bone Works. Beyond them can be seen the houses on the Brow.

Clifton Hall Farm, Rock Savage, c. 1900. If you look across the Weaver Valley from the Quay, you can see the village of Clifton. The ruined masonry is all that then remained of Rock Savage, seat of the powerful Savage family. Members of that family had included Thomas, Archbishop of York and Sir John Savage, who commanded the left wing of the Tudor army at the Battle of Bosworth Field in 1485. John Savage, Earl Rivers was a prominent Royalist during the Civil War. When Halton Castle (of which he was Constable) was captured by the Parliamentarians, his splendid residence was "unroofed" and never recovered its former splendour.

Opposite above: Crewood Hall, Kingsley. Crewood Hall commemorated its 750th Anniversary in 1990. It was the home of Gilbert Gerrard, a staunch Parliamentarian during the Civil War and to-day the Local History Group's President, Alan Waterworth resides there.

Opposite below: Aston Lodge, Aston, c. 1900. A prominent Royalist in this area was Sir Thomas Aston who lived at "Aston Hall". Aston Hall was only demolished during this century. The Aston's descendants bearing the name Talbot, now live in Aston Lodge.

Coronation Party at Seven Houses, Frodsham Bridge, June 1953. The houses were built to accommodate workers at the nearby salt works. Despite the name, there were only six of them, because the end house was a double one, probably for the foreman. They were demolished some years ago and the area became semi-derelict. A new housing development has taken place here.

Two

Churches

Frodsham parish church before the War Memorial was moved into the churchyard. The original site is now the church carpark.

Frodsham parish church, *c.* 1870. At a meeting, presided over by the Vicar, the Revd Henry B. Blogg, held in December 1879 in the Grammar School, Overton, it was unanimously decided to restore the church. The cost was over £10,000 and the work, which included an extension to the Burial Ground, took three years to complete. This is how the church looked prior to restoration. It closed after services on Sunday, 27 June 1880.

The Parish Church Nativity Play, 1948

Frodsham parish church, *c.* 1900. The church, restoration completed, re-opened for Divine Worship on St. Andrew's Day, 30 November 1882. The work, people said at the time, far exceeded their most sanguine expectations.

Frodsham Clergy in the 1890s. Here is the Rev. Canon HB Blogg with two of his curates. He was instrumental in the restoration of the parish church. On the left, the Rev. Alfred Reynolds, and on the right the Rev. Alfred Grier stand outside the front door of the old Vicarage.

The Revd Dr Miles Weight Myres, DD, FSA FR Hist S c. 1920. Dr Myres succeeded Canon Blogg in 1912 and remained Vicar of Frodsham until 1955. It has been said of him, "He was a quiet and dignified man, much respected for his scholarship. He served the parish well and faithfully for 42 years."

Herbert Hale, Lay Reader. He served in the parish church during Dr Myres' incumbency.

Two Choir Boys of St Laurence parish church.

Frodsham parish church choir at the time of Revd Noel Green's incumbency. The Church Wardens (one at each side) are (left) Mr. Forster and (right) Mr. Hurst.

The Iron Church, Main Street, c. 1880. While the parish church was closed, a prefabricated iron church was erected in Main Street. This proved unexpectedly popular, as many people, particularly the elderly, were saved the tiring climb up to Overton from the village below. It still exists and remains in use up to the present time.

Frodsham Sunday Schools, c. 1930. Each year the various Frodsham Sunday Schools competed for a Challenge Banner. Here we have a group of scholars proudly bearing their banner which they will retain for the next 12 months.

Revd Gostick's Retirement Party, Trinity Methodist Church, High Street in 1942. The Revd Gostick was the minister at Trinity for a number of years.

The Chapel at the National Children's Home, Newton. This chapel was used for many years. By the children and staff of the National Children's home until it closed in 1985.

Trinity Methodist church, High Street. Sadly, Trinity church has now been demolished, apart from the splendid spire which was saved by public donations from the people of Frodsham. A housing development called Trinity Gardens has sprung up on the site

Union church, Bridge Lane. A group of Congregationalists and Baptists in Frodsham Bridge established a Sunday School and later a chapel at the end of the nineteenth century. They first used to meet in Sutton Mills, owned by Thomas Rigby, who also financed the building of the church on the site of the old Saddle Inn in Bridge Lane. The hurch was scheduled for closure in July 2005.

Pupils and teachers of the Union church Sunday School about to set out on an outing, c. 1895. The Chapel was erected in 1886 at a cost of £2,000. It is built in red brick with a turret and a spire. It was enlarged in 1913 at a cost of £400 with seating for three hundred people.

A Bazaar in the Union church, 27 November 1912.

Five Crosses Methodist church. Methodists in the Five Crosses area had been worshipping at the old chapel in Bradley Lane for a quarter of a century, when they decided the time had come for them to move into larger premises. The building of the new chapel was carried out during the superintendency of the Rev. Edwin Mosscrop and was officially opened on 10 September 1885 by the Revd Silvester Whitehead of Manchester. The interioir and exterior have recently been modernised

Sunday School Anniversary in Five Crosses Methodist Church. The man standing to the right of the pulpit is none other than Thomas Clarke, the 1906 Scholarship Winner!

Helsby church extension, 1909. In 1909 an extension was made to Helsby church of the South Aisle, Lady Chapel (formerly called the Morning Chapel) and the porch, by J.G. Davies and Company, all by public subscription.

Three

Schools

Boys & girls of the Infants' School, c. 1900. Although a National School for Girls was opened in Frodsham in 1835, it was not until 1851 that an Infants' School was provided. We cannot put names to these delightful Victorian children, but we feel the picture had to be included!

Frodsham Infants, 1915. Here a class of Infants is sitting up straight to have their picture taken.

Frodsham Infants, Class I. Probably taken in the 1920s a large class of Infants showing they know how to hold pens!

Thomas Clarke, Scholarship Winner, Standard VI, Overton Boys' School, 1906. Thomas was born at Stonelea, Five Crosses on 19 April 1894. Sadly, he was not able to take up his scholarship due to his home circumstances. He eventually went to Cliff College at Calver in Derbyshire to study for entry into the Methodist Church Ministry. The outbreak of war in 1914, however, ended his religious studies and he served in the Royal Welch Fusiliers in France and then in Italy. After the war he returned to Five Crosses, obtained an appointment at the Brazilian Consulate in Liverpool and became a Local Preacher in the Methodist Church. After his marriage in 1929, he changed jobs and went to work for Joseph Chadwick & Sons in Warrington, where he continued for the rest of his life. The couple moved to Grappenhall to be nearer his job. A son, Thomas Malcolm Clarke, was born there in 1929. Thomas senior died in September 1960.

A class at Frodsham Boys' School, Overton in 1935. Back row, left to right: Ron Thomas, Hector Frodsham, Harry Smith, Hector Lawless, Dennis Vernon, Ted Garner, Jack Britland, Bill Turner, George Percival, Jim Percival, Rowland Shelbourne (Teacher). Third row: Godfrey Randles, Keith Davies, Eddy Eccleshall, Les Finnerty, John Kendrick, Francis Rhaney, George Fletcher, Alf Nield, Bill Fletcher, Les Vernon. Second row: George Hulmes, Tom Wade, Dennis Aston, Len Worrall, Frank Jenks, Ken Sutton, Norman Stubbs, Jim Corker, -?-. First row: Ron Maddock, Harry Fletcher, Ken Vernon, Reg Dimelow, Roy Clarke, Colin Bodell, Sam Fletcher.

Opposite above: Frodsham Grammar School, School Lane, Overton (built 1824). This replaced the original building in the Parish Churchyard and was itself replaced by the present building (now the Frodsham C.E. Primary School).

Opposite below: A typical class in the Girls' School in the early 1900s.

Boys and girls of Oaklands School, Vicarage Lane, c. 1945.

Five Crosses Infants, 1909. In 1875 a new Infants' School opened at the junction of Hillside Road and Manley Road Five Crosses, with 86 children who were saved the long walk down into Church Street. It is now the headquarters of the 4th Frodsham Scout Troop.

Four

Castle Park
and the Wright Family

Lawn mowing in progress at Castle Park, 1899. The horse was required to wear felt overshoes to protect the surface of the lawn!

Edward Abbott Wright (1808–1891). This photograph was taken in London in 1862. Edward Abbott Wright was a wealthy cotton manufacturer from Oldham and came of Quaker stock. He purchased "The Mansion, Gardens and Pleasure Grounds known as Park Place" by auction at the Bear's Paw on 20 June 1861 for £9,574.19s.0d and from then on the estate became known as Castle Park.

Mary Wright (née Kearsley) d.1868. Mary's Grandfather, Dr. John Kearsley, was a Magistrate in Philadelphia Pennsylvania, at the time of the American War of Independence. He was a zealous Loyalist who died in prison after being attacked and wounded by the rebels. His widow and children, including Mary's mother, returned to Sedgefield, Co. Durham, which was the family's ancestral home.

Mary Berry Weaver (*née* Wright). Despite parental disapproval at first, Mary Berry married a local Frodsham doctor, Dr. Frederick Poynton Weaver MD, and went to live in East Bank House in Bridge Lane (now Fraser House), where they produced four sons and four daughters.

Dr. Frederick Poynton Weaver. He was said to be a good doctor, but in a town as small as Frodsham, he would never make his fortune by his own efforts. When his wife received her substantial inheritance from the estate of Edward Abbott Wright, he ceased to practise and the family moved to London. Here he devoted himself to his many interests, including travel, walking, poetry and politics. He became a JP, a churchwarden and served on the boards of numerous missionary societies.

Above: The Board of the "East Bank Hen Company", 1886. When the family was still living at East Bank, three of Dr. Weaver and Mary's children formed a pocket-money earning enterprise keeping hens, selling the eggs and non-laying hens to their mother! (Left to right, Harriet Shaw Weaver, Harold Weaver and Maud). Harriet acted as Treasurer.

Right: Harriet Shaw Weaver in 1907. Despite coming from such a capitalist family, Harriet became a committed socialist and was a member of the Communist Party for many years. She was an early feminist and helped to publish a magazine called *The New Freewoman*. She financed a small publishing Company the "Egoist Press" from her own resources. She published James Joyce when no-one else would, as well as T.S. Elliot and many others. Nevertheless, she remained on friendly terms with her own family, especially her namesake, her aunt Harriet. The writer Samuel Beckett said of her, "I shall think of her when I think of goodness."

Castle Park Gardeners' Court, 1899. One of a series of photographs taken in 1899 by J Brandebourg, a professional photographer operating in Chester at that time.

Opposite above: Gardening Staff, Castle Park, 1899. At that time, no less than seven gardeners worked full time to keep the grounds immaculate. Today the park is maintained by Vale Royal Borough Council.

Opposite below: Opposite: The farm buildings, Castle Park, 1899. These buildings were erected during Edward Abbott Wright's time. When the mansion became the offices of the Runcorn Rural District Council in 1933, the farm buildings were adapted as Frodsham's Fire Station. Following the demise of the Rural District Council in 1974, a new Fire Station was built in Ship Street and the old Fire Station was then skilfully converted, by Vale Royal Council architects, into attractive housing accommodation for the elderly .

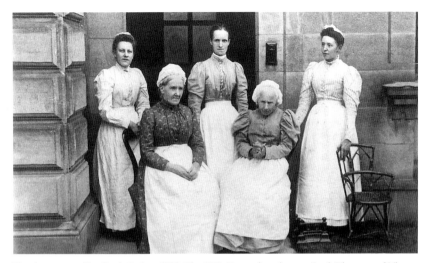

The domestic staff at Castle Park in 1899. The 1891 Census lists these as Sarah Thompson (66) Housemaid, Jane Black (60) Cook, Mary Stephenson (26) Parlour Maid, Elizabeth Hurst (31) Under Housemaid, and Mary Garnett (35) Sick Nurse. She was probably there because Edward Abbott was in his final illness at the time.

The lake, Castle Park, c. 1930. This attractive feature of Castle Park disappeared during the late 1950's due to the amount of water-pumping on the marsh for land drainage purposes and from boreholes for water supply. It is now Castle Park's carpark.

Julia Lees Garratt (*née* Wright) - The second Wright daughter to marry was Julia Lees Wright. She experienced even stronger parental objection when she wished to become engaged to a young solicitor named George Garratt, and in desperation she eloped, climbing out of her bedroom window by means of the traditional knotted bedsheets! Eventually Edward Abbott relented and the erring daughter was accepted back into the fold and went to live at Stapleton House, provided for her by her father.

Major George H. Garratt, outside Stapleton House, c. 1900. The son of Julia and George in his uniform at the time of the Boer War. His son, Stephen Garratt tells us his father and his two brothers were members of the Volunteer Company of the Cheshire Regiment. They were equipped with the necessary horses, batmen and a letter of introduction to a General from his mother, who also presented the Drill Hall to Frodsham.

Stapleton House, *c.* 1900. The home of the Garratt family. Sadly, this splendid Victorian building no longer exists and has been replaced by three modern detached houses.

The staff at Stapleton House, *c.* 1900. Only two of these appear to have lived in. They were Annie Darlington (28), Cook, and Mary Hopley (24), Housemaid. We assume the others were local people.

Five

Personalities

Thomas Riley and family, 1911. Kelly's Directory for Frodsham, 1892 describes Thomas Riley as "Registrar of Births, Marriages & Deaths, Relieving Officer, Registrar for Marriages for Runcorn, and School Attendance Officer", but he was much more. He was the Secretary to the Gas Company, Collector of Rates & Taxes, Secretary to the Frodsham Permanent Building Society, and agent for the Northern Fire & Life Assurance Co. He was the Church Organist for much of his life and also a churchwarden. A veritable "Pooh-Bah!"

John Pollard, Headmaster, Frodsham Endowed Boys' School, 1854–1898. John Pollard began his long career as headmaster at a salary of £50 per annum but with a house and garden provided. He was a fine schoolmaster and it is said he did not possess a cane although he did have a walking stick which he sometimes used on recalcitrant scholars!

Mrs. Elizabeth Pollard (née Chadwick). John Pollard's wife was Elizabeth Chadwick of Todmorden in Lancashire. For a few years, Mrs Pollard served as headmistress of the Girls' School, but resigned to bring up a family of seven children. Two of their sons, Arthur Edwin and Leonard became Pollard Brothers, Drapers.

Dr. John Frodsham Robinson, c. 1890. The elder brother of James Frodsham Robinson, the chemist and naturalist. He was a lifelong bachelor and lived in what is now the last house in High Street before the Catholic Church. The Robinson window in the Kingsley Chapel of Frodsham Church is dedicated to him and his sister. It is said that the face of St. Paul in this window is based upon that of Dr John, who had been a churchwarden. The rood screen was also erected in his memory.

Joseph Gilmour Kydd, c. 1900. Born in Coleraine, Northern Ireland, he was apprenticed to a Liverpool grocer in 1878 and came to Frodsham to manage the firm's shop, which he eventually bought. He established a second grocery store which he called Frodsham Co-operative Stores to answer competition posed by the Runcorn & Widnes Co-op opening a shop in the town. He also built the jam works at the top of Sandfields, called Kydd & Kydd, the management of which was handed to two of his brothers.

Frederick Hough (and son) in their pony and trap, *c.* 1900. Hough's had a painting and decorating firm in Frodsham for many years. At that time a pony and trap was the equivalent of the family car and it was a common sight in Frodsham.

The Cotgreaves with their pony and trap, *c.* 1930. Cotgreaves were butchers in Frodsham who still used a pony and trap throughout the war years when petrol was all but unobtainable.

Sergeant George Farrall of the Volunteers (Cheshire Regiment) *c.* 1900. George was a crack shot and won many trophies for marksmanship. We see him with his rifle and the trophies he won using it.

"Water" Bob Rodgers and sons, dressed for the Carnival, *c.* 1930. Bob Rodgers earned his nickname because he was the foreman in charge of Frodsham's water supply and sewerage. It also differentiated him from his contemporary "Tailor" Bob Rodgers! In his youth he took part in the traditional Soul Caking play and could still remember it word for word many years later. He obviously enjoyed dressing up!

Left: Fred Holland, Road Foreman, *c.* 1920. As County Council Road Foreman, Fred was provided with a motorcycle to travel round the district. He was the world's slowest motorcyclist and used frequently to be overtaken by push bikes! The story (probably apocryphal) goes that one day he came on to a site on foot and a workman said "Hullo, Fred, has your motorcycle broken down?" "Oh no," said Fred, "I was in a bit of a hurry to get here, so I left it at home!"

Below: Mr and Mrs Joe Rigby and granddaughter Christine, *c.* 1949. Joe was a wheelwright with his premises on the main road at Frodsham Bridge near the Bridge Inn.

Above: Joe Barker, Artist, *c.* 1970. For many years, Joe Barker followed his hobby of collecting old photographs of Frodsham, thereby building up a wonderful visual record of the village from the earliest days of photography up to comparatively recent times. He later took up painting to record buildings and scenes of old Frodsham which no longer exist. His death was a sad loss to the village.

Right: Billy Tweedle, *c.* 1880. Billy Tweedle was the "sand man" who used to sell sand he excavated from the Manley Road caves, which at that time was used for spreading on cottage floors.

Sir William Crossley. This photograph taken from a painting is of the wealthy engineer William Crossley who designed oil and gas engines, much used for water and sewage pumping stations. His home was Ravelstone in Manley and he founded the Crossley Sanatorium nearby for the treatment of the terrible scourge of consumption (as tuberculosis was called in those pre-antibiotic days).

Joseph Martin. A native of Frodsham who at the age of 15 emigrated to the United States, where he made a fortune in the ice and cold-storage business. At the height of his career he was known as the "Ice King of California." In his will he left $5,000 to create a charitable trust for the poor of Frodsham. This was used to build the Joseph Martin Nurses' Home at the junction of Kingsway and Martin Road.

A Victorian Wedding in Frodsham. They were serious affairs in those days!

Frodsham's oldest inhabitants in 1907. Front row, left to right: A Jones (81), K Ainsworth (82), M Jones (83), E Davies (94), E Turner (89), E Garner (84). Back row: E Roberts (86), J Miller (82), T Jones (84), J Harrison (87), S Vernon (84), J Ellison (80), P Illidge (83).

The Wedding of Joseph & Martha Ellams of Helsby, *c.* 1920.

The Davies Family of Rose Farm, Helsby, 1905. The Davies family donkey cart in the stack yard at Rose Farm, left to right; Mrs Davies, Helena, Edward, Peers & Annie Lewis. Peers, the "baby", now lives in the Pensioners' Bungalows in Mountain View, Helsby.

Six

Occupations and Trade

Thomas Rigby & Son's Flour Mill at Frodsham Bridge, 1 May 1915. Grain came to the mills by barge. There was a grain elevator capable of lifting 60 tons per hour from the hold of a barge to the top floor of the mill. The flour was distributed by teams of splendid horses, as we see here, and later by Foden Steam wagons.

Horses and cart outside Stapleton House, c. 1900. The carter seated on the wall on the right was Edward Jones, who lived in the cottages in Mill Lane, Frodsham Bridge, next to the Aston Arms. Mr. Jones was responsible for a team of five horses, although only three are in use in the photograph. They were watered before setting out at the pump in Mill Lane and this stop outside Stapleton House, after the long pull up Fluin Lane, was their first rest on the way to Kingsley Mill.

Foden Steam Wagons at Rigby's Mill, Frodsham Bridge, c. 1915. These impressive (and powerful) steam wagons superseded the horses and carts during the First World War. They were manufactured at Sandbach in Cheshire after Fodens won a competition organized by the War Office for a military steam wagon and they were much used by the army at that time.

Thomas & Hannah Chantler, Basket Makers, c. 1900. The Chantlers lived in a cottage adjoining the Railway Inn in Church Street. It is possible that William Bibby senior worked for Thomas Chantler when he first came to Frodsham from Warrington before he set up his own business.

William Bibby & Sons' Basket Works, c. 1904. This photograph, taken when Bibby's occupied the premises at the rear of Church Street, backing on to Alvanley Terrace shows William Bibby senior, his son (also William), grandson, John Edward Bibby and their workmen. The baskets shown are potato hampers which formed the bulk of their production although many other types of basket were produced.

Work in progress at Five Crosses Smithy, c.1900. Frederick Houghton, blacksmith, giving his orders to his men engaged in re-shoeing a pony.

Price (and sons) Fish Cart, Ashley Gardens, c.1900. Grocers, bakers, butchers and other tradesmen were prepared to deliver straight to your door in those days. Here Fishmonger Price is delivering to his customers in Marsh Lane.

Above: Spraying fruit bushes in Bibby's orchard in the 1920s. Francis Bibby pumps while Gerald Abram does the spraying. Part of the orchard became the site of St. Luke's Primary School (previously Orchard House Infants School 1970–1993). Fluin Lane can be seen in the background.

Right: Dennis France, Barber, at work in the 1970s. Dennis came to his barber's shop in High Street just after the Second World War and continued in business for 40 years. The shop was once part of Gorst's, a mini Department Store in the early 1890s and early 1900s. It is now three separate businesses.

Ashworths also used Foden Steam Wagons. Driver Pettinger (shown in this picture) was later killed when his head collided with a telegraph pole as he looked out in the dark. The man on the left with the dog is George Rodgers (Ashworth's foreman) who subsequently kept the Railway Inn in Church Street.

Kingsley Windmill, c.1900. This turn of the century photograph is viewed across the ornamental pond, tennis court and grounds of Crofton Lodge. It was owned by John Gibson, who came to Kingsley from Warrington. Today nothing of the mill can be seen, but the adjoining houses are still known as Windmill Terrace. Another Gibson, Alfred, owned the water mill in Mill Lane.

Shops, Main Street, *c.* 1900. At this time T Pover "Tobacco & Cigars" occupied the shops. In 1908 Sarah Hayes from Ship Street moved in and let the shop at the right hand end to Mrs Holland who ran a sweet shop. The left hand end comprised the living quarters and the centre became the new chip shop. Chip shops were beginning to spring up in towns in the north-west and Frodsham's became an immediate success. It lasted for over 80 years.

The shop of J Moss, Clogger & Boot Repairer, Church Street, *c.* 1890. "Clogger Moss" had his shop in what is now the rear of the Golden Lion. His clogs were made in the traditional way and there was a healthy demand for them in Frodsham. Sadly, the building was destroyed by fire in 1902 and the Golden Lion was extended over the site.

Ann Trude, Millinery & Gowns, Church Street, *c.* 1930. A bit higher up Church Street was Ann Trude's shop which catered for quite a different clientel than "Clogger Moss", as is evident from her window display!

Peter Booth, Shoe Retailer & Outfitter, Church Street, *c.* 1930. Peter Booth's double-fronted shop was situated in the row of shops between Kydd's Wynt and the white cottage occupied by the Bibby's.

Above: S Hancock, Family Butcher, Church Street *c.* 1930. This shop was built as a butcher's, but is now used as the Cheshire Building Society's office. Note the telephone number Frodsham 17.

Right: Runcorn & Widnes Industrial Co-operative Society's Grocery Shop, High Street, late 1930s. Since the emergence of Supermarkets, the Co-ops are no longer such a major force in food retailing. The site of this shop has now been engulfed by Somerfields, but is now, by a strange irony, a Co-op supermarket.

JG Kydd & Co, Grocers & Provision Merchants, Church Street, in the late 1930s. Kydd's at this time was the epitome of a successful grocer's shop, using no less than three modern delivery vans. The plethora of advertisements is interesting, but I doubt whether the Planning Authority would approve these days!

Opposite above: JG Kydd & Co, Grocers Shop (Internal) in the late 1930s. It was one of the busiest shops in the village, selling everything from Choice Empire Butter to "Perfection" soap, from Wine and Spirits to "Skyscraper Cocktails". The grocery business was taken over by a Liverpool firm before closing down in the mid-seventies. It is now a wine bar.

Opposite below: Kydd & Kydd's Jam Works in course of demolition, 1973. One of JG Kydd's enterprises, built in 1891 at the top of Sandfields. It was called "Kydd & Kydd" because he handed over its management to two of his brothers. They died soon afterwards and their widows sold out to the Liverpool firm of Morris & Jones. Production continued here until the late 1950's, when the works was closed down. The site was sold and re-developed with three-storey town houses in 1973.

Sailing ships under tow on the Manchester Ship Canal off Frodsham Marsh, c. 1900. Two small schooners towed by an MSC steam tug. Such vessels were granted free towage to the port of Runcorn because the construction of the canal made navigating a sailing ship on the waterway difficult. Sailing flats (or barges) were also a common sight at this time and the sails of two of them can be seen in the distance.

Salt Port at the confluence of the River Weaver and the Ship Canal, c. 1890. Prior to the completion of the Ship Canal, a temporary port was established where ships could discharge cargoes. Here it is under construction.

Runcorn Bone Works, Clifton. There were two undertakings alongside the River Weaver at Frodsham Bridge which used bones as a raw material to manufacture glues, gelatine and fertilisers – Joseph Ashworth & Sons and Heywood & Massie. When Heywood & Massie closed down the tanks used for processing the bones are believed to have been transferred to this works at Clifton, which is no longer in operation.

Frodsham Mineral Water Company. Two cousins by the name of Ellison and Corker founded a mineral water company in 1888. It was behind Mill Bank Cottages, off Main Street. It was re-named Frodsham Mineral Water Co. in 1912 and many of their old bottles with "glass alleys" in the neck still remain. The man holding the horse is Joe Ellison, a son of the founder and the boy on the cart, Billy Booth.

Laying electricity cables in Fluin Lane, *c.*1912. The Mersey Power Company was set up to supply electricity to the Castner Kellner Works and the Salt Union at Weston Point. The company only began to supply power to domestic consumers in 1912, so this was certainly one of the first electricity cables to be laid in Frodsham.

Frodsham Fire Brigade, 1930. Back row, left to right: Jack Pritchard, Frank Bennison, Richard Forster, William Gleave, Thomas Ellams and Arthur Hutchinson (whose taxi they used). Front row: Charlie Rogers, Tommy Langwine, Ted Fletcher (Captain), Walter Lawless (Chairman), Joe Berry, Jack Carter and John William Percival.

Frodsham Station, c. 1900. The railway station was a busy and thriving establishment when the twentieth century dawned. Cattle, potatoes, cheese and all manner of agricultural produce was exported through the goods yard. There were also sidings at the top of Station Road and a busy commuter service ran to Liverpool, Chester and Manchester.

Frodsham Station Platform Staff in the early years of the century. Standing beneath the long lost canopy is the Station Master, ticket clerks, porters and boys. A far cry from present staffing levels.

Frodsham Railway Goods Yard Staff. Almost as many as Platform Staff. A job on the railway was a life-time's career in those days.

Railway delivery vehicle, Frodsham Railway Goods Yard, c. 1930. Left to right: Harry Bell, ? Griffiths, Ted Blythe.

Helsby Cable Works at noon, c. 1910. Workmen streaming out of the main gate at Helsby Works at lunch time. There are very few women to be seen. Notice the sign which reads "HELSBY TYRE WORKS". The Company decided to take up the manufacture of motor car tyres in 1905 and even installed a motor car tyre test-track, but it was not successful and production ceased in 1912.

B.I. Cables Senior Management, c. 1900. In the front row (2nd and 3rd from the left) can be seen the two brothers, James Taylor and George Crosland Taylor who founded B.I. Cables in Helsby.

Seven

Sport and Leisure Activities

Frodsham Scouts dressed to perform the traditional Soul Caking Play in the 1930s – This was a revival of Frodsham's ancient annual rite. It was based on a Mummers play and was common (in various versions) all over the country. The First World War seems to have killed off Soul Caking in Cheshire, although the Comberbach Soul Cakers have managed to keep it alive up to the present time.

Ces Bate and Ted Birtles. Two stalwarts of Scouting in Frodsham, who kept the 1st Frodsham Troop going through the years of the First World War and expanded it in the years which followed. Both served as Scoutmaster in their turn. Their joint services to Scouting amounted to more than 100 years and their dedication was legendary.

The Mayoress throws a dart for Scout funds, probably in the 1930s.

1st Frodsham Boy Scouts Troop, *c.* 1910. The troop was started by Mr Charlie Hutton in 1909 and it has survived ever since. Their uniform was a green shirt with a sky-blue neckerchief. For camp they borrowed a hand cart and pulled and pushed it to camp at Delamere. It's uphill out of Frodsham which ever way you go.

1st Frodsham Scout Troop on Parade in Church Street, Coronation Celebrations, June 1953 – 44 years since their inauguration and still going strong!

Scout Troop at the Union Church, Bridge Lane. These boys include Charlie Carrington, Jack Morgan, Jack Smith, Barrie Berrington, Edwin Clarke, Norman Berry, Frank Bell and Cyril Berry.

King George V's Visit to Frodsham, 8th July 1925. The King, accompanied by Lord Derby and Sir William Bromley Davenport visited Frodsham on his way from Knowsley to the Royal Show at Chester. He was received by Mr James Illidge, Chairman of the Parish Council and Major JG Ashton the Rural District Council Clerk. He is seen inspecting the local Girl Guides Boy Scouts and over 300 ex-Servicemen.

Frodsham Girl Guides in the 1940s. There have been Guides in Frodsham as well as Scouts since the early 1900s. They were started by Dr. Selby's wife assisted by Dr Selby's daughter Barbara and Kathleen Cooper of Bradley. They first camped under canvas at Hatchmere. Back row, left to right: Jean Ryder, Marjorie Ainsworth, Janice Allman, June Tudor, Doreen Dykes and Margaret Land. Third row: Margaret Ellams, Diane Davies, Gillian Charnley, Margaret Hughes, Inez Peplow, Iris Bell, Ruth Pendlebury and Mrs. Phyllis Butterworth. Second row: Barbara Hill, Margaret Bell, Nancy Faulkner, Mary Hancock, Nancy Nield, Marian Dimelow, Shiela Forster, Judy Fletcher, Anne Fletcher and Jean Lewis. Front row: Betty Thomas, Sylvia Lockett, Dorothy Moss, Joan Shingler, Ivy Lightfoot, Joan Frodsham, Helen Fletcher and Joan Lewis.

Frodsham Volunteers' Band, *c.* 1890. The Volunteers were the equivalent of today's Territorial Army and the Frodsham Company was an important element in the village at that time. There was a Volunteer Company of the Cheshire Regiment which fought in the Boer War and included many local men. There is a memorial to them in the Parish Church.

Frodsham Subscription Band, 1909. With the demise of the Volunteers, a Subscription Band was established about 1907. Three generations of the Ellison family were associated with Frodsham Bands and John George Ellison (in bowler hat in the centre) was the Bandmaster of this one. His sons, Fred (5th from left on back row) and Harry (the young boy on the right of the front row) were also members.

Frodsham Silver Band in the 1930s. By 1916 the band had become known as Frodsham Silver Band. They were equipped with uniforms and better instruments and were very much in demand for all kinds of functions in the area. John's son Fred took over as Bandmaster in 1930 until he died in 1948. Fred's son, John Ellison was much involved in Scouting and almost inevitably he eventually took over the Scout Band.

Frodsham Silver Band on Parade in Church Street in the 1930s.

Tom Turner's Dance Orchestra, c. 1920/30. Tom Turner plays the piano, Harry Jones (a local painter and decorator) plays the bass, with Tommy Langwine on the drums. The Ellison family are represented (of course!) by John G. Ellison on the piccolo and his son Fred on the cornet.

The Grand Cinema Orchestra in the days of silent films. Tom Fylde, the Cinema Manager is conductor, Fred Ellison plays the cornet, Harry Jones on the bass and Charlie Boyers (who became Manager at the Co-op) on the cello. The drummer and violinist are not known.

Frodsham Morris Dancers, c. 1923. This troupe of Morris Dancers performed to raise funds for the repair of St. Laurence's Church Organ. Cecil Rogers, Phyllis Hughes, George Harrison, -?-, Percy Jones, -?-, ? Jones, Jim Tudor, Norah Bibby, Fred Norcross, Kathleen Williams, Jack Bibby, Francis Bibby, Doris Unsworth, Phyllis Guest, Alice Rodgers, Bob Gleave and Bill Jackson.

Ladies Country Dancing in Frodsham in the early 1930s. This Folk Dancing Group was trained by Norah Britland (née Guest) who lived on Hollybank. Most members of the group were teachers from Runcorn Schools. The photograph was taken at a performance on the lawn at the rear of Trinity church.

A Frodsham Players Christmas Party in the 1940s. The Players were formed during the Second World War. Back row, left to right: Florence Connor, Robert Burnett, Enid Jones, Robert Lewis, Clifford Way, Doris Greenleaves, Bertha Shelbourne, Gwyneth Littler, Walter Evison. Middle row: Vera Evison, Kathryn Hill, Roland Benson, Leonard Norman, William Kingrewe, Josephine Hutchings, Frederick Kirkbride, Winifred Hough, Jean Barraclough. Sitting: Joan Laurence, Laura Plummer, Muriel Woodier, Madeleine Tedbury, Maurice Kay, Fay Kay, Edith Yould, Margaret McNaughton. In front: Rowland Shelbourne and John Smith.

Fancy Dress Bazaar in the Skating Rink, Bellemonte, *c.* 1900.

FRODSHAM CHORAL SOCIETY'S BALL. FEB. 4th 1914.

Frodsham Choral Society Ball, 14 February 1914. Held in the Drill Hall in Main Street, this was probably the last one before the outbreak of the First World War and the Society seems not to have survived afterwards.

A well-attended Whist Drive in the Parish Room, Moor Lane in 1912.

Mothers' Meeting Tea in the Victoria Room, Chapel Lane on Friday evening, 28 April 1893.
We think the seated lady is Julia Lees Garratt of Stapleton House.

Edith Fletcher, Helsby Rose Queen, 1910. A Rose Queen was elected every year to adorn the festivities of the annual Rose Fête. There is a series of photographs, but we have chosen Edith to represent them all.

The child Characters behind Helsby C.E. School, Helsby Rose Fête, 1911. The competitors assemble to have their photograph taken before setting off in procession through the village. Notice particularly the 1911 aeronaut!

Characters – Helsby Rose Fête, 1912. The following year the children are lining up to set off from the school to the Fête.

A line of Sailor Boys for Helsby Rose Fête, c.1905. Left to right: Edward Davies, Harold Bibby, Tom Hodgkinson, ? Bazley, Harold Bellingaul(?), Hubert Fairhurst, Harold Davies, John Barnes, Les Harrison and Joe Worrall.

Helsby Band leading the Procession, Helsby Fête, 1909. Rose Farm can be seen on the left. There was no problem about stopping the traffic in those days!

At the bottom of the Helter-skelter, Mersey View in the 1930s. Good value at a penny a go! The slide was wax-polished and on the opening day it was used no less than 3,600 times!

A decorated float in Frodsham Carnival in the 1920s. The two ladies are Mesdames T Corker and T Fylde.

The Fancy Dress Parade, Frodsham Carnival, 1929.

Frodsham Rose Queen, c. 1931. Rose Queen Joan Thompson attired in a red velvet cloak surrounded by her retinue. The picture was taken in the garden of Mrs. Fylde in Kingsway. She was the wife of Tom Fylde, the manager of the Grand Cinema.

Carnival King & Queen in Main Street, in the 1930s. A King and Queen were elected for each carnival and here we see them in Peter Snelson's landau.

An open-air boxing match, c. 1890s. This is a mystery photograph. We have no details of where, or when, this took place, nor the names of the contestants, except that it was somewhere in the Frodsham area. It is not bare-fisted and there is a referee and seconds, but no ring!

Lady Tennis Players in Frodsham – These ladies used to play on a site at Mersey View. Florence Davies, who started the club, persuaded Mrs. Parker-Hoose to rent them some land. Florence insisted that no men must be allowed to play there! Back Row: Elizabeth Such & Beatrice Birtles. Middle Row: Annie Davies, Emily Davies, -?-, Mary Dobson, Norah Guest & Florence Davies. Sitting on the grass: Maud Such & Mary Davies.

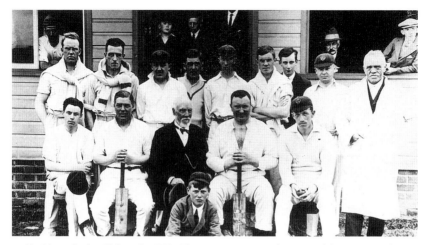

Frodsham Cricket Club in the 1930s. This was very active at the time and the venue was down Moor Lane which is still called Cricket Field Lane by many of the older generation. At the right-hand end of the front row is Frodsham's demon bowler, Harry Tudor, who worked in the Rating Department of the Rural District Council, Castle Park.

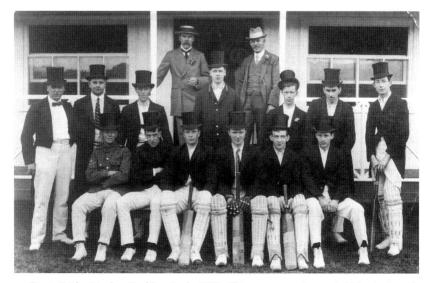

Comic Cricket Match at Frodsham in the 1920s. This was an annual event, held for charity and on this occasion it was a top hat and tails occasion!

The Liverpool District Cup arrives at Helsby Station, 1908. Helsby AFC won the Liverpool District Cup in the 1907/08 Season and here it is being welcomed on arrival at Helsby Station by supporters of the club.

Overton Boys' School First Eleven Football Team in the 1920s. The Boys' School had several very successful teams in the 1920s and this is one of them. Back row, left to right: Syd Berrington, Len Farrell, ? Capper, Arthur Booth, Billy Walker, Alfred Evans, Joe Berrington and Rubin Jones. Middle row: ? Deane, Wilf Ellams and Bill Hayes. Front Row: Charlie Hopley, Barrie Berrington, Alec Clarke, Billy Moores and Ronnie Lazenby.

Frodsham AFC Team and Officials 1913/14. This must have been the most successful of the Frodsham Club's teams, with their trophies on display. Back row, left to right: Richard Forster, Henry Russell, Tom Corker, -?-, ? Hughes, -?-, Fred Clarke, -?-, -?-, ? Brennan, Llewellyn Davies, -?-, Jophn Wilkinson, Robert Jones, Albert Bromiley and Tom Turner. Front row: Frank Russell, Norman Spencer, ? Hughes, -?-, Harry Frodsham, Harry Savage and Percy Jones. Left side: Tom Langwine, -?-. Right side: Sidney Spencer and Wilmot Baines.

Frodsham Golf Course. This consisted of nine holes and was situated on land between Hazlehurst Road, Manley Road and Crowmere Lane. The caves were in these fields. The club was formed about 1900 and most local businessmen, teachers and clergy were members. The Rev RL Mann was Secretary in 1910. It ceased to exist about 1918.

Frodsham's St. John's Ambulance Brigade in the inter-War years.

Charabanc Outing about to leave the Golden Lion, *c.* 1920. "Water Bob" Rodgers, wearing a large flat cap, stands at the extreme left of the group. The two boys in Eton collars inside the bus are George Murray and Arthur Forster, son of Harry Forster, Landlord of the Golden Lion.

Allotment holders, Park Lane/Princeway area, 1918.

The Ladies' Race, Frodsham Sports Day, 1933. Held on the football field behind the gasworks in what is now called Greenfield Lane, left to right: Florence Worrall, Mrs Littler (née Andrews), Mrs Thomas, -?-, Mrs Jones, Mrs Norcross, Mrs Mallion, Netta Massey, Mrs Bodell and Mrs Lightfoot. Bob Smith hovers in the background!

Frodsham Wildfowlers off for a day's sport on Frodsham Marsh. Frodsham had a large and active Wildfowlers' Club, who used to shoot, not only over the Marshes, but across the Manchester Ship Canal on Frodsham Score.

Eight

Wartime

The Unveiling of Helsby's War Memorial, 25 April 1920. Helsby's War Memorial takes the form of a Celtic Cross with the names of the dead listed round the plinth. There are 20 names for 1914/18 and 17 for 1939/45.

Patients and Nurses at the Red Cross Hospital, Helsby, c. 1916. During the First World War, the B.I. Recreation Hall ("The Rec") in Britannia Road was taken over as a Red Cross Hospital. The firm had been using X-rays to discover faults in cables and X-ray equipment, which was not at all common at that time, was made for use by the hospital.

Patients, Nurses (and a Donkey) at Helsby Red Cross Hospital. We are not completely certain of the date of this photograph, but if the flags are anything to go by, perhaps it was November 1918 and victory was being celebrated.

Patients and Nurses at Frodsham Auxiliary Hospital, *c.* 1916. The Skating Rink Bellemonte Road was taken over as an Auxiliary Military Hospital. The Medical Officer was Dr. Blades Ellison, who lived in Brentwood, Red Lane. From March 1915 to 1919 no less than 3,435 patients from all parts of the Empire were treated.

Frodsham Ladies' Committee, the Drill Hall, *c.* 1918. The Ladies' Committee organized comforts for the troops during the First World War. We see them seated outside the Drill Hall Gates in Main Street.

Helsby Village Home Guard No.3 Platoon outside B.I. Cable Works, Helsby, *c.* 1941. Front row: ? Pennington, RAF: Sgt.Henry Monks, Lt. George Rushton, Lt. Walter Britland, Sgt. Harry Holland, George Hughes RN. Middle Row: Joseph Wilson, George Matthews, Geoff Monks, Joe Ellison, -?-, Fred Crewe, -?-, -?-, ? Clegg, Jeff Hughes , Tom Neal, Bert Barnes, Edwin Boyle, Bert Fletcher, Bill Thomas, Lee Wild, Tony Rushton, Gordon Thomas, -?-. Back row: -?-, Russell Barnes, -?-, G Wilson, Harry Lightfoot, ? Shaw, Evan Ellams, H Ward, Tom Partridge, Bert Bu'lock, Les Yates, -?-, Marshal Lea, -?-.

Frodsham's No.1 Platoon Home Guard, Frodsham Gasworks, *c.* 1942. Commanding Officer, Lieut. Large.